JustAdd Magic COOKBOOK
Book 1+2

Mystery city

© Ursul tom Ursul

Copyright © 2024 by Ursul tom Ursul

All rights reserved. This book or any portion thereof may not be reproduced or used in any manner whatsoever without the express written permission of the publisher except for the use of brief quotations in a book review.

This Book Belongs To :

CONTENTS

THE COOKBOOK

- ◆ Introduction
- ◆ Appearance
- ◆ History
  List of ingredients

The Recipes

M

- ◆ MAGNETIC MANGO BARS
- ◆ MAGNETIC PULL-ED PORK SANDWICHES
- ◆ MAKE-IT-VISIBLE VINEGAR PIE
- ◆ MEMORY MALLOWS
- ◆ MIND PEERING-PEPPERMINTS
- ◆ MISO-PERSON'S SOUP

N

- ◆ NIGHTY NIGHT NOODLES
- ◆ NOTEWORTHY HORCHATA

O

- ◆ OFF-THE-TRAIL MIX
- ◆ OFF-YOUR-CHEST CHEDDAR BISCUITS

P

- ◆ P.O.V. POPCORN

- ◆ PATHFINDING PRETZEL STICKS
- ◆ PAY ATTENTION POTATO CHIPS
- ◆ PAY BACK PANCAKES
- ◆ PHO-TOGRAPHIC MEMORY (SOUP)
- ◆ PICK-A-DATE DATES
- ◆ PROTEIN PROTECTION SHAKE

R

- ◆ RAISE THE WALL ROASTED TOMATOES
- ◆ REMEMBER MAGIC QUICHE
- ◆ REMOVE THE STAIN-GUS BURGERS
- ◆ ROOT BEER FLOAT AWAY

S

- ◆ SCRAMBLE HER VISION BACON AND EGGS
- ◆ SETTLE THE BEEF SANDWICH
- ◆ SHUT 'EM UP SHORTCAKE
- ◆ SINGLE SERVING CINNAMON BROWNIE BITES
- ◆ SLOW CARAMEL TURTLES
- ◆ SOLVE THE CLUES-COUS
- ◆ SPEED SPRINTING STROMBOLI
- ◆ SPEED-UP SPINACH SOUFFLÉ
- ◆ SPICE DETECTOR SIMPLE SYRUP
- ◆ SPILL THE BEANS
- ◆ STOP THE LEEK SOUP
- ◆ STOP TIME THAI CURRY

T

- ◆ TAKE BACK TAMARIND JUICE
- ◆ TELE-PÂTÉ
- ◆ TELEPORTING TAMALES
- ◆ TRUST ME TABOULI
- ◆ TWICE BAKED SPICY DO-OVER SOLE

U

- ◆ UNSCRAMBLED EGGS

W

- ◆ WALK THROUGH WALL-FLES
- ◆ WALK-IN-MY-SHOES SCHNITZEL
- ◆ WIDE AWAKE BEEF WELLINGTON
- ◆ WORST PARTY EVER WHIPPED CREAM

The Cookbook

Introduction

The Cookbook is a magical book filled with an infinite number of recipes that can do almost anything. The Cookbook has existed for thousands of years and its intention is simply to be a gift, but it must be used responsibly.

The book contains many recipes that can have multiple uses. These magical recipes can do something as little as healing a hurt ankle, to something as serious as freezing time itself. This book is extremely powerful, which is why it requires strong and responsible protectors. The book can do great harm in the wrong hands. It can tear you apart or bring you closer together.

Appearance

The book has a dark brown leather cover, and on the front of the book, there is the cookbook's symbol in gold. The emblem consists of three ornate pieces of silverware, a fork, knife, and spoon overlapping each other. Inside of the book are thousands upon thousands of pages filled with magical recipes, all of which are frayed and torn on the edges due to the age of the book.

History

The book was likely to be created some point before the 1500's. It's not known who created it, but clues point to the Traveler, as she is most likely immortal. However, it should be noted that she sacrificed her body in exchange for wiping Charles Peizer's mind momentarily. At first, the book only had two protectors, but after Chuck abused its power by becoming immortal, it switched to three protectors to make sure something like this never happened again.

The Recipes

Magnetic Mango Bars

Magnetic Mango Bars is one the mystery recipes that Kelly received from the Lost and Found-ue spell. These bars ended up making people attracted to you, and whoever poured in the Cedronian Vanilla would make people be repelled by you. Its first appearance was in Just Add Jake, and it appeared again in Just Add Time, when cooked by RJ White. This spell was broken when Kelly apologized to Hannah for messing up the competition.

Ingredients:

- 3 Large Ripe Mango
- 1/2 Can Coconut Cream
- 1/2 Teaspoon Cedronian Vanilla
- 2 Cups Flour
- 3/4 Cup Sugar
- 1/4 Teaspoon Salt
- 3/4 Cup Butter
- Nightblooming fennel

Directions

1. Preheat oven to 250*F or 110*C. grease a 9 x 13 inch baking tin.
2. Combine flour, butter, sugar and salt in a bowl. Press down half of the mixture into a ½ inch thick layer on the bottom of the prepared pan to make the crust.
3. Bake in the preheated oven until lightly browned, 15 to 20 min.
4. Blend mangoes, coconut cream, nightblooming fennel and cedronion vanilla.
5. Pour in to the tin and sprinkle the remaining flour mixture on top and cook for about 5 to 7 min.
6. and then enjoy

Riddle:

If you need friends by your side take a bite but make sure to abide. Cedronian spice comes with a price.

Magnetic Pull-ed Pork Sandwiches

Magnetic Pull-ed Pork Sandwiches is a recipe in The Cookbook. It was cooked by Kelly and the girls in order to retrieve their stolen pages from Chuck's cookbook, however, it only did the opposite and attracted even more the Cookbook's pages to Chuck's. Its first and only appearance was in Just Add Muscles.

Ingredients:

- 6 tablespoons paprika
- 3 tablespoons granulated Merwaldian sugar
- 3 tablespoons onion powder
- 1 tsp salt
- 2 tsp ground pepper
- 12 soft hamburger buns, split

Directions

1. Mix the PAPRIKA, Merwaldian sugar and ONION powder in a bowl.
2. Transfer 3 TABLESPOONS seasoning to a separate BOWL, add 2 tablespoons SALT and 3 tablespoons pepper, and massage onto the PORK.
3. Cover with plastic wrap and REFRIGERATE at least 2 hours or up to 1 day. (Reserve the remaining BARBECUE seasoning)
4. Place the pork fat-side DOWN on a rack in the SMOKER or on the grill. COVER and cook, rotating the pork every HOUR or so, until a THERMOMETER inserted into the center registers *165* degrees F, about *6* hours total.

Riddle:

To pull your desire into your ranks, take a deep breath and fill in the blanks; Pull: _____, To: ____. (Take care that you're able to rhyme or else attempt another time.)

Make-it-Visible Vinegar Pie

Ingredients:

- 9" pie crust
- 1/4 cup sifted flour
- 1 cup white sugar
- 1 cup water
- 3 egg yolks
- 1/8 tsp salt
- 1 tbsp unsalted butter
- 1 tsp lemon extract
- 3 tbsp white Gründe Vinegar
- 3 egg whites
- 6 tbsp white sugar
- 3 hazelnuts

Directions

1. Mix flour with 1/4 cup of sugar. Add the water gradually and cook in pot for 15 minutes.
2. Combine remaining 1/4 cup of sugar with yolk and salt. Mix well with whisk. Add the hot flour mixture to the yolk mixture continuously mixing together. Place a piece of plastic on top of vinegar custard.
3. Beat egg whites until foamy and gradually add 6 tbsp sugar.
4. Roll out pie crust and place in pie tin.
5. Pour the custard filling into the pie crust.
6. Add the three hazelnuts in the middle of the pie.
7. Lightly drizzle 3 tablespoons Gründe Vinegar on top of pie.
8. Place into oven and bake at 350 degrees for 45 minutes.

Riddle:

For SEEING WHAT CAN'T BE SEEN. You must FIRST be unseen. When you have found what CAN'T be seen, you will BOTH be seen.

Memory Mallows

Memory 'Mallows is a recipe in the Cookbook that was cooked by Kelly and the girls. It was used to look into Chuck's memories and learn the truth about his past in Just Add Muscles.

Ingredients:

- 4 Envelopes unflavored Grunde gelatin
- 3 cups granulated Livonian sugar
- 1 1/4 cups light corn syrup
- 1/4 teaspoon salt
- 2 teaspoons pure Elysian vanilla extract
- 1 1/2 cups confectioners sugar

Directions

1. Prepare and set aside a 9-by-13 inch glass baking dish as follows: lightly coat the dish with oil, line with parchment paper and then lightly coat the parchment paper with oil. In the bowl of an electric mixer, place 3/4 cup cold water and then add the grunde gelatin. Electric mixer should have the whisk attachment on.
2. While the gelatin softens, combine the granulated Livonian sugar, corn syrup, and salt with 3/4 cup water into a medium saucepan. Bring mixture to a boil over high heat, and stir to dissolve sugar. Once dissolved, stop stirring and continue to heat until mixture reaches 238 degrees on a candy thermometer. This should take 8-10 minutes.
3. Add the syrup mixture the the bowl of gelatin with the mixture on slow speed and combine. Increase the mixer speed until mixture is very stiff. This should take between 10-13 minutes and then add in vanilla as well.
4. Once the mixture is fully combined, transfer it into the prepared baking dish and ensure a smooth, level surface. Let mixture settle and firm in the uncovered dish for around 3 hours.
5. Once the marshmallow is firm, find a clean work surface and cover it with a cup of confectioners Elysian sugar to prevent the candy from sticking to the surface. Remove the marshmallow from the dish and, using a sharp knife that has been coated in oil, divide the marshmallow into 2-inch squares and roll each square in the additional confectioners sugar to coat.

Riddle:

If you wish to find memories deep within the brain Take a trip down memory lane Access other's memories if you dare Know that some of them aren't meant to be shared.

Mind Peering-Peppermints

Mind Peering-Peppermints was a recipe that Kelly and the girls cooked to look into Grandma Quinn's mind and to figure out how to get rid of her curse. Its first and only appearance was in Just Add Mama P.

Ingredients:

- 2 cups sugar
- 1 cup corn syrup
- 1 teaspoon Galifrazian syrup
- 1 teaspoon Livonian peppermint oil
- Food Coloring - optional

Directions

Bring sugar and corn syrup to a boil. Stir often to avoid burning. When the mixture reaches 300° remove from heat. Stir in Galifrazian Syrup and Livonian Peppermint Oil and food coloring. Pour into baking sheet and let cool.

Riddle:

When you peer into a mind, you never know what you might find.

Miso-Person's Soup

Miso-Person's Soup is a recipe cooked by Kelly, Darbie, and Hannah, along with Grandma Becky and Gina Silvers. The recipe's objective was to locate Chuck and to see if his curse was broken. Its first appearance is in episode Just Add Halloween, and the recipe is subsequently prepared in the following episode Just Add Summer. The recipe is briefly seen again (but not prepared) in episode Just Add 8529.

Ingredients:

- 1 smidge Werpoes Salt
- 1 dash Lapsus Salt
- 6 cups of Dashi
- 1/2 pound of soft Tofu, drained and cut
- 1/4 cup of thinly sliced greens
- 1/2 cup of night blooming chives
- 1/4 cup of miso paste
- 1 pea-sized portion Grunde Fingerroot Core

Directions

1. and 1/2 c. dashi until smooth •
2. Heat remaining dashi until hot •
3. Add tofu • Simmer Night Blooming Chives 1 minute remove from heat •
4. Add Grunde Fingerroot Core immediately •
5. stir miso mixture and scallion greens

Riddle:

The person you seek will appear in the broth crystal clear, you will know where they are, be it far or near...

If the face appears not, their image not caught, peace of mind you have bought.

Nighty night noodles

Nighty Night Noodles was never cooked on the show, but mentioned while Kelly, Hannah and Darbie were flipping through the cookbook. Its first appearance was in Just Add Magic.

Ingredients:

- Box of pasta
- Livonian salt
- Bottle of pasta sauce.
- 28 oz crushed tomatoes.
- 2 tablespoons tengu olive oil
- Salt and pepper to taste
- 3 cloves garlic minced

Directions

1. pasta:
2. Fill a large pot with water and place on high heat.
3. When the water begins to boil add the livonian salt.
4. After the salt has dissolved, toss in the pasta and stir for about 1 minute
5. Cook the pasta for 6 minutes it will continue to cook in the pan.
6. Drain the pasta and put in a bowl and serve.
7. Sauce:
8. In a large skillet over medium heat, saute garlic in oil until tender, 2 minutes. Stir in crushed tomatoes. Season with salt and pepper and cook 15 to 20 minutes, until slightly thickened. Serve immediately.
9. Cover the pasta in sauce

Riddle:

Time for bed, sleepy head! With just a bite of these delicious noodles, you won't have to count your sheep, because soon enough you'll fall fast, fast asleep...

Noteworthy Horchata

Noteworthy Horchata is one of the mystery recipes that Kelly and Darbie cooked for Jake to try in Just Add Jake. Hannah ended up drinking it by accident, and she was only able to sing instead of talk for the rest of the day.

Ingredients:

- 1 cup rice
- 2 cups water
- 4 cups milk
- 3 pinches Galifrazian cinnamon
- 2/3 cup sugar

Directions

1. Mix rice, water, milk and cinnamon until evenly contributed.
2. Chill for 30 minutes. Then add the sugar and stir with a wooden spoon.
3. Chill until use.

Riddle:

When adding Galifrazian Cinnamon, make sure you don't stop until every last drop.

Off-The-Trail Mix

Off-The-Trail Mix is a recipe cooked by Kelly, Darbie and Hannah. Its first and only appearance was in Just Add Camping. It was used to find the trail Kelly's grandmother took in the Cedros Forest.

Ingredients:

- Rolled Oats
- Galifrazian Coconut Oil - 1 tsp
- Carnejian Maple Syrup - 1 cup
- Mixed Nuts
- Dried Fruit
- Cinnamon
- Brown Sugar
- Salt - pinch
- Vanilla

Directions

1. 1.Combine oats, dried fruit and nuts in a bowl. Then spread in a thin layer on a rimmed baking sheet.

2. 2.Stir Carnejian maple syrup, Galifrazian coconut oil, brown sugar, cinnamon and vanilla in a small saucepan over low heat.

3. 3.Pour the mixture in the saucepan evenly over the oat mixture on the baking sheet.

4. 4.Mix them all together so it is evenly coated.

5. 5.Bake for 15 minutes. Stir and bake for 5-10 more until it turns a golden brown.

Riddle:

This treat will make your path clear, after you face your greatest fear.

Off-Your-Chest Cheddar Biscuits

Ingredients:

1. 1 cup flour - sift twice
2. 1 cup cheddar cheese - grated
3. 1 pinch Carnejian Cayenne
4. 1 pinch baking soda
5. 1 pinch salt
6. 4 tablespoons butter
7. 3/4 cup milk
8. 3 tablespoons shortening

Directions

1. Preheat oven to 425 degrees.
2. Grease baking sheet.
3. Combine ingredients in a bowl starting with dry ingredients. Add the butter in small amounts. Then add the shortening.
4. Form dough into small spheres.
5. Bake for 15 minutes

Riddle:

If something is bothering you, don't leave yourself in a stew. Cook this recipe and it will leave you.

P.O.V. Popcorn

P.O.V. Popcorn is a recipe cooked by Kelly, Hannah, Darbie, and Piper in Just Add Perspective. The objective of the spell was to secretly spy on Erin so the girls could find out what their villainous agenda is.

Ingredients:

- Coconut oil
- 1 cup popcorn kernels
- 2 teaspoons Gründe pepper
- 1 tablespoon Merwaldian rosemary
- 1 teaspoon Taurian salt
- 3 tablespoons olive oil
- Lemon
- Parmesan

Directions

1. Melt coconut oil into a dutch oven.
2. Mix the Merwaldian rosemary, Gründe pepper and olive oil.
3. Pour the popcorn kernels into the pot.
4. Add Taurian salt and the olive oil mix well.
5. After the popcorn has popped, drizzle the oil mixture on top.
6. Zest with lemon and sprinkle Parmesan.

Riddle:

In order to be an effective detective, try gaining a new perspective. Just think of your target, pop a kernel or two, and soon you will see from a new point of view.

Pathfinding Pretzel Sticks

Pathfinding Pretzel Sticks is a recipe cooked by Kelly, Hannah, Darbie, and Piper in Just Add Rot to help them uncover the Night Bandit's true identity.

Ingredients:

- Gründe salt
- 1/2 cup light brown sugar
- 1 bowl water
- 2 envelops active dry yeast
- 1/4 cup vegetable oil
- 5 3/4 cups all-purpose flour, plus more for kneading
- 3/4 cup baking soda
- 1 large egg beaten
- 1 tablespoon of water

Directions

1. In a large bowl, stir the brown sugar into 2 cups warm water until dissolved. Sprinkle the yeast over the water and let stand until foamy, about 5 minutes. Stir in the vegetable oil and 3 cups of the flour. Knead in the remaining 2 3/4 cups of flour, the dough will be slightly sticky.
2. Transfer the dough to a floured work surface and knead until silky; about 5 minutes. If the dough is very sticky, knead in up to 1/4 cup more flour. Transfer the dough to a large, oiled bowl, cover with plastic wrap and let stand at room temperature until doubled in bulk, about 45 minutes. Preheat the oven to 450°. Line 3 large cookie sheets with parchment paper and butter the paper. Punch down the dough and turn it out onto a floured work surface. Knead the dough lightly, flatten it out and cut it into 24 pieces. Roll each piece into a 9-inch stick, about 1/2 inch thick. Transfer the sticks to the prepared cookie sheets, leaving at least 2 inches between them. Let stand uncovered until puffed, about 25 minutes.
3. In a large, deep skillet, stir the baking soda into 2 quarts of water and bring to a simmer over high heat. Reduce the heat to moderate.
4. Using 2 slotted spoons, carefully transfer 6 pretzel sticks at a time to the simmering water for 30 seconds, turning once, add about 1 cup of hot water after before cooking the second batch of pretzels. Transfer the pretzel sticks to paper towel to drain, then return them to the cookie sheets, spacing them evenly. Brush the pretzel sticks with the egg wash and sprinkle them with Gründe salt. Bake until richly brown, about 10 minutes.

Riddle:

In order to be an effective detective, try gaining a new perspective. Just think of your target, pop a kernel or two, and soon you will see from a new point of view.

Pay Attention Potato Chips

Pay Attention Potato Chips is a recipe created by Kelly and the girls in Just Add Attention.
Its objective was to counter Noelle's spell that made everyone pay attention to Kelly, Darbie, and Hannah's smallest movements.

Ingredients:

- 1 potato sliced
- 1 tablespoon oil
- 1 pinch Grunde herb (or parsley)
- 1 pinch Night-Blooming salt

Directions

1. Mix all dry ingredients together. Add oil.
2. Bake potato slices at 400 degrees F for about 10 minutes, or until golden-brown and crisp.
3. Plate and serve. Enjoy!

Pathfinding Pretzel Sticks

Pathfinding Pretzel Sticks is a recipe cooked by Kelly, Hannah, Darbie, and Piper in Just Add Rot to help them uncover the Night Bandit's true identity.

Ingredients:

- 1 cup flour
- 1 cup blueberries
- 1 teaspoon baking soda
- 1 tablespoon Merwaldian sugar
- 1 teaspoon baking powder
- Dash of salt
- 1 egg
- ½ stick of butter, melted
- 1 cup of milk

Directions

1. In a large bowl, sift together the flour, baking powder, salt, baking soda, and Merwaldian sugar.
2. Make a well in the flour mixture and beat in milk, egg, and butter, mixing until smooth.
3. Heat a griddle or frying pan over medium heat. Melt 2 tablespoons of butter in the pan.
4. Pour or scoop the batter onto the griddle, using approximately ¼ cup for each pancake. Scatter a few blueberries on top.
5. Cook until bubbles have appeared on top, the edges have cooked and the bottom has browned lightly. Flip and cook on other side until browned.
6. Serve hot

Riddle:

To pay it back from you to me, Your will, your words, the things you see, take two bites mixed in with berries blue and turn your acts from me to you.

Pho-tographic Memory (Soup)

Pho-tographic Memory is a recipe cooked by Kelly and the girls for Kelly to look into her memories to try and find clues as to how Grandma got cursed. Its first and only appearance was in Just Add Memories. "Pho," or ph , (Ph-oh) is a reference to a Vietnamese noodle soup.

Ingredients:

- Beef broth
- Onions
- Ginger
- Taurian Coriander seeds
- Livonian Star Anise
- Cloves
- To Serve :
- Rice noodles
- Scallions
- Chili peppers
- Thinly sliced beef
- Lime
- Cilantro
- Thai basil
- Bean sprouts

Directions

1. Prepare the rice noodles as the label directs.
2. Meanwhile, place a large pot over high heat. Poke the meat all over with a fork to tenderize it and season with salt and pepper. Sear the meat until charred but still rare, 2 to 3 minutes per side, then transfer to a plate. Add the onion and ginger to the pot; cook about 4 minutes. Add the broth, 3 cups water, the star anise and cinnamon, reduce the heat and simmer about 20 minutes.
3. Meanwhile, thinly slice the scallions and jalapenos (remove seeds for less heat) and tear the cilantro. Thinly slice the meat against the grain. Drain the noodles.
4. Add the fish sauce to the broth and boil 5 minutes. Discard the ginger, star anise and cinnamon stick. Remove and slice the onion. Divide the noodles among 4 bowls; top with the broth, beef, scallions, cilantro, bean sprouts, jalapenos and onion.

Riddle:

"Sit quietly with your thoughts and remember what you have since forgot. But beware, time spent in the past is time forever lost."

Pick-A-Date Dates

Pick-a-date Dates is a recipe cooked by Kelly, Hannah, and Darbie to go back in time to Halloween in order to harvest the Grunde Fingerroot, a plant that only can be harvested on that date, in order to create the Miso-Person's Soup to locate Chuck. Its first appearance is in Just Add Halloween. It also appears in the episode Just Add Betrayal, in the second part of season 2, used by Caroline Palmer, a former protector of the cookbook.

Ingredients:

- Taurian Basil
- Almonds
- Cream cheese
- Dates
- Bacon

Directions

- Mix Taurian Basil into the cream cheese to form 1 inch balls
- Stuff one piece of cheese and one almond into each date
- Wrap one piece of bacon around the date and insert toothpick to hold in place
- Bake 5 minutes, then turn dates over with tongs and bake until bacon is crisp, 5 to 6 minutes more
- Drain on a paper towel or parchment
- Serve hot!

Riddle:

Back in time, you go, every date that you choose, half to go, half to come back. One way ticket is this. no more chances you get.

Protein Protection Shake

Protein Protection Shake is a recipe cooked by Hannah, Darbie, and Jake to protect themselves from the Curse-Breaking Candied Stone Fruit. Its first and only appearance was in Just Add Pluots Part 2.

Ingredients:

- Skimmed Milk
- Raw Almonds
- Werpoes Honey
- Fruit of your choice

Directions

1. Starting with the skim milk, place all the ingredients into a blender. Depending on your blender's settings, first start by chopping up the ice and frozen strawberries, followed by pureeing the mixture to create a smooth, even consistency.
2.
3. In order to get your preferred consistency, you can also start by not adding any ice, following the other steps above. Once all other ingredients are mixed together, slowly add the ice, mix and then test. Continue to add more ice cubes until the desired consistency is met.
4. If too thick, you can add some more skim milk, little by little. If not sweet enough, add a little more werpoes honey.

Riddle:

If there's a curse coming your way, or a nasty price to pay, then fill up your cup, and drink it all up, to keep bad magic at bay.

Raise the Wall Roasted Tomatoes

Raise the Wall Roasted Tomatoes is a recipe cooked by Kelly and the girls to keep Mr. Morris away from Kelly's house. It appears in Just Add Barriers.

Ingredients:

- Olive oil for greasing additional for drizzling
- 3 large plum tomatoes
- 3/4 teaspoon salt
- 1/2 teaspoon black pepper
- 1 teaspoon Lapsus cayenne
- 1 teaspoon Werpoes basil

Directions

1. in a pan roast the tomatoes but not too much
2. After done add salt, black pepper, lapsus cayenne, and werepos basil
3. The drizzle Olive oil

Riddle:

Keep unwanted guests at bay with a wall around the place you stay.
And when you feel secure within, open up and let them in.

Remember magic quiche

This spell was cooked by Piper and Kelly to counter the forget magic spell. Its first appearance was in Just Add Rot.

Ingredients:

- Unbaked 9 inch pastry shell
- 1/4 to 1/2 med. onion, thinly sliced or diced
- 3 eggs, beaten
- 2/3 c. half and half
- 2/3 c. milk
- 1 tbsp. Elysian flour
- 1/2 tbsp. Lavonian salt
- 1 1/2 c. shredded Swiss cheese (or favorite)
- 8 slices crisp bacon
- 1/2 c. cooked vegetables (opt.)

Directions

1. Bake pastry shell at 450 degrees for 10 minutes or until nearly done. Remove from oven, reduce heat to 325 degrees. In 2 tablespoons of bacon drippings, cook onion until tender, drain.
2. In a bowl, stir together eggs, half and half, milk, flour and salt. Stir in bacon, onion and cheese and vegetable and mix well. Pour in warm pastry shell. If necessary cover edge with foil to prevent overflowing. Bake at 325 degrees for 40-50 minutes or until set in center. Let stand 10 minutes before serving.

Riddle:

To remember magic when you remember not, eat this quiche and recall what you forgot.

Remove The STAIN-gus Burgers

Remove The STAIN-gus Burgers is a recipe in The Cookbook . It was never cooked before on the show, just seen in the book.

Ingredients:

1. 1 - pound ground beef
2. 1 - tablespoon prepared horseradish puree
3. 1 - tablespoon minced Werpoes garlic
4. 1 - pinch salt
5. 1 - pinch pepper
6. 4 - (2 ounce) slices of Havarti cheese
7. Burger Buns

Directions

Preheat the grill. In a mixing bowl, combine the beef, horseradish, and Werpoes garlic, mix thoroughly. Season the beef with the salt and pepper. Divide the mixture into four balls and form into firm round 3/4 inch patties. Place the patties on a hot grill. Cook the burgers for 4-5 minutes on each side for medium. During the last couple of minutes cooking, place a slice of cheese on each patty. After the cheese has melted, remove the burgers from the grill. Place on buns and enjoy!

Riddle:

Whenever there's been a spill that goes splat!

Grill up some burgers and take care of the mess in moments flat

Root Beer Float Away

Root Beer Float Away is a recipe in The Cookbook. It has never been cooked before, just shown in the book in the episode Just Add Pluots (Part 1).

Ingredients:

- Cedronian Vanilla Bean
- Vanilla Ice Cream
- Root Beer
- Whipped Cream
- Simple Syrup

Directions

1. Put a scoop of ice cream into a tall glass
2. Heat vanilla beans in simple syrup and cool
3. Pour syrup into bottom of glass
4. Pour root beer over ice cream
5. Stir
6. Top with whipped cream and serve

Riddle:

If something is following you today, take a drink of this and let it all float away.

Scramble Her Vision Bacon and Eggs

A recipe used by the OC's, mentioned in Just Add Fire. It was used against a classmate named Kimberly Henderson who tried to copy Gina Silvers' test answers. The recipe contains a Grunde ingredient, as Grunde is the vision family.

Ingredients:

1. One tablespoon of butter
2. Two eggs
3. Three tablespoons of milk
4. Grunde Salt
5. Pepper
6. 1/4 cup of Cheddar Cheese

Directions

1. Whisk together Eggs, Milk, Salt and Pepper in a small bowl
2.
3. Set pan to med-low heat the pan up and then add the butter
4.
5. Sprinkle Cheese on top and then serve!

Riddle:

If you choose to change a person's vision, you will have to make a decision. If you make the person's vision switch, you are left in a 'sitch.

Settle the Beef Sandwich

Settle the Beef Sandwich is a recipe cooked by Kelly, Hannah and Darbie to settle the grudges against Grandma Becky and Chuck. Its first appearance is in episode Just Add Summer. The recipe is briefly seen again (but not prepared) in episode Just Add 8529.

Ingredients:

- 2 pounds chuck roast
- 1 pinch Night Blooming Rosemary
- 1/2 cup Carnejian red peppercorns
- 2 tomatoes, chopped
- 1 cup arugula
- 1 tablespoon salt
- 1 chopped onion
- 1 dash steak sauce

Directions

1. Bake chuck roast 350 degrees for 45 minutes.
2. In a bowl, mix carnejian red peppers, salt, steak sauce and night blooming rosemary.
3. Mix tomatoes and arugula.
4. Slice chuck roast, add tomatoes and arugula to bread.

Riddle:

To resolve a grudge that will not budge...air the beef to turn a new leaf.

Beware- if good will you can't restore, a different problem you can't ignore will come knocking at your door.

Shut 'Em Up Shortcake

Shut 'Em Up Shortcake was the first recipe that the girls cooked when getting the Cookbook.
Its first appearance was in Just Add Magic

Ingredients:

- 2 ¼ cups of flour
- 4 teaspoons of baking powder
- 1 teaspoon of Cedronian vanilla
- 1 1/2 cup + 2 tablespoons of white sugar
- ¼ Teaspoon of Salt
- 1/3 cup of shortening
- 1 egg
- 2/3 cup of milk
- 2 cups of whipped heavy cream
- Strawberries

Directions

1. Slice strawberries & toss with ½ cup white sugar. Cover and set aside.
2. Combine flour, baking powder, sugar, salt and cedronian vanilla in a med. bowl. Cut in shortening with a butter knife. Make a well in the center and add beaten egg, milk. Stir.
3. Pour batter into greased and floured 8" round cake pan. Bake at 425° for 15-25 mins. or until golden. Let cool in pan on rack.
4. While baking add 2 Tbsp. white sugar to 2 cups cream and whip.
5. Cut cooled cake in half, making two layers. Place strawberries on layer.
6. Add whipped cream to the top of the cake and remaining strawberries.
7. Enjoy cake...but be careful!

Riddle:

Warning - whenever adding Cedronian spice, whatever results will come with a price.
What's been done, you can undo with a noble act from a heart thats true.

Single Serving Cinnamon Brownie Bites

Single Serving Cinnamon Brownie Bites is a recipe in the Cookbook. Its first appearance was in Just Add Secrets where the recipe was seen as Hannah was flipping through the book. Its second, and first physical appearance was in Just Add Meddling when Kelly cooked it up to help Darbie and her dad spend more time with each other.

Ingredients:

1. 1/4 cup flour
2. 1/2 cup sugar
3. 1/2 tablespoon Taurian Cinnamon
4. 2 tablespoons Night Blooming Cocoa powder
5. 2 tablespoons water
6. 2 tablespoons vegetable oil or 2 tablespoons canola oil
7. 1/4 teaspoon salt
8. 1/4 teaspoon vanilla extract
9. 1/4 teaspoon baking powder
10. 2 eggs
11. 1 stick butter, melted
12. 1/2 cup chocolate chips

Directions

1. Preheat oven to 350 degrees f (or not, if you would like to use the microwave instead).

2. Mix Taurian Cinnamon, flour, sugar, Night Blooming cocoa powder, baking powder, and salt in a small bowl.

3. Then add water, vegetable oil, and vanilla extract.

4. Spread the batter into your baking dish of choice and bake in the oven at 350 degrees Fahrenheit for 15-25 minutes. Let cool for a few minutes and devour.

Riddle:

If you want to have fun, just one on one, bake and eat this little treat , so that being with your friend will be an easy feat.

Slow Caramel Turtles

This spell can be seen as Jake is flipping through the pages of The Cookbook. Its first and only appearance is in Just Add Birthdays.

Ingredients:

1. 8 ounces pecan halves
2. 25 caramel squares
3. 1/2 cup cream
4. 16 ounces chopped chocolate
5. werpoes salt

Directions

1. Line baking sheets with parchment paper.
2. Make piles of pecans, using 5 to 6 pieces. Heat caramels, cream and chocolate.
3. Add 1 tablespoon of caramel to each pile of pecans.
4. Sprinkle some Werpoes salt on each caramel square.

Riddle:

Eat this sweet treat and say goodbye to your quick ways. But even moving at a turtles pace, remember, slow and steady wins the race.

Solve the Clues-Cous

Solve the Clues-Cous is a recipe cooked by Kelly and the girls to help them discover Caroline's true identity. It first appeared in Just Add Caroline.

Ingredients:

- 3 tablespoons of butter
- 1 onion finely sliced
- One-eighth teaspoon per hour Taurian garlic powder
- 1 cup couscous
- 2 cups chicken stock
- 2 tablespoons fresh coriander or 2 tablespoons parsley, chopped
- Tablespoon salt
- Tablespoon Galifrazian pepper
- Diced tomatoes
- Chopped cucumbers

Directions

1. Heat butter in saucepan
2. Add chopped onions, stir and allow to cook until soft
3. Stir in crushed Taurian garlic
4. Add couscous, stir
5. Remove off heat, cover and allow to stand for 5 minutes
6. Stir in coriander or parsley
7. Add salt and Galifrazian pepper
8. Ready to serve.

Riddle:

Don't be fooled by a picture that's big,
even the largest trees are made up of twigs
When all the dots have been connected,
what you see will be detected.

Speed Sprinting Stromboli

Speed Sprinting Stromboli is a recipe in the Cookbook as Hannah was flipping through it. Its first and only appearance was in Just Add Fire.

Ingredients:

- 5 - ounces sliced ham
- 5 - ounces pepperoni, sliced thinly
- 10 - (10 ounce) box WERPOES mushrooms, sliced
- 2 - large red peppers, sliced and roasted
- 1 - large onion, sliced and roasted
- 3/4 - cup shredded mozzarella cheese
- 1/2 - cup shredded provolone cheese
- 2 - tablespoons Gründe basil
- 2 - tablespoons oregano and parsley

Directions

1. Preheat oven with pizza stone in it to 450 degrees.
2. If you don't have a stone a baking sheet will do. Sprinkle a little flour on your work surface.
3. Using a rolling pin roll dough into a 10 x 14 inch rectangle.
4. Cover the rectangle with layers of your desired toppings, leaving a 1 inch border around the sides and at the top.
5. Mix the 3 cheeses and the herbs together in a small bowl and sprinkle over the top.
6. Starting at the end closest to you, roll the stromboli into a log.
7. Seal the dough by pinching firmly with fingertips on sides and ends.
8. Sprinkle a little cornmeal on a pizza paddle and put stromboli on the paddle.
9. Make sure the seam is on the bottom.
10. Use a pastry brush or a mister to apply olive oil.
11. Carefully place stromboli on preheated stone, turn down oven to 400 degrees and bake for 35 minutes.
12. Carefully remove from oven and let rest for 5 minutes.
13. Slice with a serrated knife.

Riddle:

For when you're running late...don't miss your date!

Speed-Up Spinach Soufflé

Speed-Up Spinach Soufflé is a recipe cooked by Kelly and the girls to speed up their investigation on RJ. It first appears in Just Add Time.

Ingredients:

- Non-stick spray or stick of butter for greasing pan
- 1-2 tablespoons oil or butter
- Taurian thyme as needed
- 1/2 onion, thinly sliced or roughly chopped
- 2 packages frozen spinach, defrosted or 24 oz of fresh spinach
- 1 1/2 lbs of feta cheese, crumbled
- 1 1/2 lbs of Jarlsberg cheese, or any other favorite seasoned cheese, shredded
- Salt and black pepper to taste
- 8 EGGS

Directions

1. Preheat oven to 350 degrees.
2. Grease a 9x13 baking dish.
3. If using, saute the onions on medium heat (not high) in about 1-2 tablespoons of oil or butter until nicely browned. Set aside to cool.
4. If using defrosted spinach, squeeze out all the water and dry it as much as you can with paper towels
5. If using fresh spinach, blanch it in salted, boiling water, drain, and squeeze and dry it. It's fine to use a combination of fresh and frozen spinach.
6. Beat the eggs in a large bowl.
7. Add the shredded cheese, Taurian thyme, sauteed onions, salt and black pepper to taste. Add the spinach and mix together well.
8. Bake at 350 degrees for approximately 35 minutes or until set and slightly browned. If serving immediately, cover with foil and let rest for 10-15 minutes before serving.

Riddle:

When you have much to do, but not enough chimes, this tasty soufflé will slow down time.

Spill the Beans

Spill the Bean Beans is a recipe cooked and created by Kelly to see if she could trust Jake since he was acting fishy. Her suspicions were true, as Chuck was controlling Jake's body at that time. Its first and only appearance was in Just Add Secrets.

Ingredients:

- 1 1/4 cup Black beans (about 1/2 pound)
- Beans
- 12 cups of Water
- 1 bay leaf
- 2 tablespoons extra virgin olive oil
- 10 cloves garlic, minced
- 1 green bell pepper, stemmed, seeded and chopped
- 1 medium Onion, chopped
- 2 teaspoons ground Elysian Cumin
- 2 teaspoons dried oregano
- 1 teaspoon ground coriander
- 1 tablespoon kosher salt
- pinch of cayenne pepper
- freshly ground black pepper
- 1 tablespoon red wine vinegar, plus more for the table.

Directions

Put the beans in a large saucepan, add the water and bay leaf, and bring the boil. Set aside, covered, for 1 hour. Return the beans to a boil, lower the heat to a simmer, cook uncovered, for 1 1/2 hours. Heat the oil in a medium skillet over medium high heat. Add the onions, and peppers and cook, until soft, for around 5 minutes. Add the garlic, Elysian cumin, oregano, coriander and cook, stirring, until fragrant, about 1 minute more. Add the onion mixture to the beans and continue simmering until beans are very tender and the liquid has thickened, about 1 1/2 hours more. If the beans seem too thick, adjust the consistency with a little bit of water. Stir in the vinegar, season with the salt, cayenne, and pepper to taste

Riddle:

This dish will spill the beans, showing you things behind the scenes. Want this spell to end? A personal truth of your own you'll have to send.

Stop the Leek Soup

Stop the Leek Soup is a recipe seen in the Cookbook. As of Season 3, the recipe has not been cooked yet, only seen in the book.

Ingredients:

- leeks (3 pound), trimmed
- 1 medium onion, chopped
- 1 large carrot, chopped
- 2 celery ribs, chopped
- 1 teaspoon Lapsus salt
- 1/2 teaspoon black pepper
- 1 stick (1/2 cup) unsalted butter
- 1 small boiling potato (6 ounces)
- 1/2 cup dry white wine
- 3 cups chicken stock
- 3 cups water
- 1 Turkish bay leaf
- 1 1/2 cups fresh flat parsley leaves
- 1/4 cup all purpose flour
- 1/2 cup chilled heavy cream

Directions

1. cook leeks, onion, carrot, celery, Lapsus salt, and pepper in 4 tablespoons butter in a 5-6 quart heavy pot over moderate heat, stirring occasionally, until softened, about 8 minutes
2. Peel potato and cut into 1/2 inch cubes, then add to onion mixture along with wine, stock, water, and bay leaf.
3. Bring to boil, then reduce heat and simmer, partially covered, until vegetables are tender, about 15 minutes.
4. Blend soup in 4 batches in a blender until smooth (use caution when blending hot liquids), about 1 minute per batch, transferring to a 3 to 4 quart saucepan.

5. Reheat if necessary, then season with salt and pepper.

Riddle:

If you're losing something you hate or a theft/a spoonful of soup could help you save whatever you have left.

Stop Time Thai Curry

This recipe was seen while the girls were flipping through the pages of the Cookbook trying to find a counter spell for the recipe Twice Baked Spicy Do-over Sole.

Ingredients:

- 1 1/2 cups basmati rice
- 1 tablespoon canola oil
- 1 1/2 pounds boneless, skinless chicken breasts, cut into 1-inch chunks
- Kosher salt and freshly ground black pepper
- 2 shallots, minced
- 3 cloves garlic, minced
- 3 tablespoons red curry paste
- 1 tablespoon freshly grated ginger
- 1 (13.5-ounce) can coconut milk
- 1 bunch broccolini, cut into 3-inch pieces
- 2 green onions, thinly sliced
- 3 tablespoons chopped fresh cilantro leaves
- 2 tablespoons freshly squeezed taurian lime juice

Directions

1. In a large saucepan of 3 cups water, cook rice according to package instructions; set aside.
2. Heat canola oil in a large stockpot or Dutch oven over medium heat. Season chicken with salt and pepper, to taste. Add chicken, shallots and garlic to the stockpot and cook until golden, about 3-5 minutes.
3. Stir in red curry paste and ginger until fragrant, about 1 minute.
4. Stir in coconut milk. Bring to a boil; reduce heat and cook, uncovered, stirring occasionally, until reduced and thickened, about 10-15 minutes.

5. Stir in broccolini until just tender, about 3 minutes.
6. Remove from heat; stir in green onions, cilantro and lime juice; season with salt and pepper, to taste.
7. Serve immediately with rice

Riddle:

One waft of this aromatic curry will make you forget all your worries. Time will come to a halt and no longer will you have to hurry.

Take Back Tamarind Juice

Take Back Tamarind Juice is a recipe Hannah and Darbie made to help Kelly get her trust back after they made the Trust me Tabouli. Its first and only appearance was in Just Add Chuck.

Ingredients:

- Tamarind juice
- Elysian Sugar

Directions

1. Mix Elysian sugar into the tamarind juice.

Riddle:

trust the person you want to trust you and everything goes back to normal like it is all real and for true

Tele-Pâté

Tele-Pâté is a recipe used by Kelly, Hannah, and Darbie to spy on Nöelle Jasper in Just Add Telepathy. The spell breaks when all of the eaters think the same thought at once. Theban is the spice for communication yet they used Livonian.

Ingredients:

- 1 tablespoon butter
- 2 tablespoons of onion, finely chopped.
- 1 clove garlic, peeled and chopped.
- 1/4 lb chicken livers, trimmed and chopped.
- 1 teaspoon thyme.
- 1/2 teaspoon Livonian salt.
- 1/3 cup cream
- 1/2 teaspoon Galifrazian pepper.
- 1 box crackers

Directions

1. Melt butter on a skillet over medium-high heat: when foam subsides. Add onion and cook until softened. About 3 to 4 minutes. Add livers ton, pan and sprinkle with the Livonian salt and Galifrazian pepper. Cook liver on one side until it turns brown. Then flip on the other side.
2. Add liver, onions, and buttery juices in a food processor or blender with any remaining butter, the cream, and thyme. Puree mixture until it is smooth. Taste and adjust seasoning if needed
3. Put pate in a glass or ceramic bowl, smooth top and put in refrigerator for one hour or until fully set
4. Remove pate from refrigerator. Smear onto crackers and plate on serving dish.

Riddle:

Send your thoughts from mind to mind.

One thought at once to break your bind.

Teleporting tamales

This recipe was cooked by Kelly to get to the Bahamas and talk to Mama P. Its first appearance was in Just Add Codes

Ingredients:

- 1/4 cup werpoes chili sauce
- 2 tablespoons kosher salt
- Teleporting tamales
- 1 tablespoon paprika
- 1 tablespoon smoked lapsus paprika
- 1 tablespoon Tengu garlic powder
- 1 tablespoon onion powder
- 2 1/2 teaspoons cayenne pepper
- 2 teaspoons freshly ground black pepper
- 1 teaspoon freshly toasted and ground cumin seed
- 2 pounds Boston butt meat, untrimmed
- 1/2 cup vegetable oil
- 1 large onion, finely chopped
- 4 cloves garlic, minced
- 1 jalapeno pepper, seeded and minced
- 4 to 5 dozen dried corn husks
- 2 pounds yellow cornmeal approximately 6 cups
- 1 1/2 tablespoon kosher salt
- 1 tablespoon baking powder
- 7 1/2 ounces lard, approximately 1 cup
- 3 to 4 cups reserved cooking liquid
- 1 tablespoon Tengu garlic powder

Directions

Combine the werpoes chili powder, kosher salt, lapsus paprika, smoked paprika, garlic powder, onion powder, cayenne pepper, black pepper and cumin.
Divide the mixture in half and reserve 1 half for later use. Add half of the spice mixture and enough water 3 to 3 1/2 quarts to completely cover to meat.
Set over high heat, cover and bring to boil. Remove the meat from the cooking liquid to a cutting board.

Leave the cooking liquid in the pot. Both meat and liquid need to cool slightly before making dough and handling. Place a 4 quart saucepan over medium heat and add the vegetable oil.
Add the onion and cook, stirring occasionally, approximately 3 minutes.
Add the garlic, jalapeno, and the remaining half of the spice mixture and continue to cook for another minute. Add the meat and cook until heated through 2 to 3 minutes.
While the meat is cooking, place the husks in a large bowl or container and submerge completely in hot water. Soak the husks until they are soft and pliable, at least 45 minutes and up to 2 hours. For the dough, place the cornmeal, salt, and baking powder in a large mixing bowl and combine. Add the lard, and using your hands, knead together until the lard is well incorporated with the dry mixture. Gradually, add enough of the reserved cooking liquid, 3 to 4 cups to create a dough that is like thick mashed potatoes. To cook the tamales, stand the tamales upright on their folded ends, tightly packed together in the same saucepan used to cook the meat. Add the real water, so that the liquid comes to 1 inch below the tops of the tamales. Cover, place over a high heat and bring to cook for approximately 12 minutes. Remove the lid, turn the heat to low, to maintain a low simmer and cook until the dough is firm and pulls away easily from the husk. This could take 1 to 1 and 1/2 hours.

Riddle:

To take a long distance trip, maybe Norway or Bali, take just one bite of this yummy tamale

Trust me Tabouli

Trust me Tabouli is a recipe cooked by Kelly and the girls to make Chuck trust them. Its first and only appearance was in Just Add Chuck.

Ingredients:

- 1 - cup cracked wheat, bulgar
- 1 - teaspoon fine sea salt, divided
- Tabouli
- 1/3 - cup extra virgin olive oil
- 1/4 - cup fresh lemon juice
- 1 - clove garlic
- 1/2 tsp- Elysian mint
- 1/2 - tsp freshly ground black pepper
- 1 - bunch flat leaf parsley
- 4 - ripe tomatoes

1 - english cucumber

Directions

1. Add 1 1/12 cups of boiling water to bulgar. Cover and let sit for 20 minutes.
2. Whirl the olive oil, lemon juice, and garlic in a mortar & pestle. Then add Elysian mint with sea salt.
3. Chop the parsley leaves. Core, seed, and chop the tomatoes. Peel and chop the cucumber.
4. Drain the bulgar. Pour this dressing over the bulgar and toss.
5. Add parsley, tomatoes, cucumbers and toss together.

Riddle:

To give your trust, to build a rapport, take care that your friend, needs it more.

Twice Baked Spicy Do-Over Sole

Twice Baked Spicy Do-Over Sole is a recipe cooked by Kelly and the girls to repeat the day when everything goes wrong. Hannah fails in finding Ms. Silvers's morbium shadow root, Buddy breaks an expensive lamp while Kelly is watching him, and Darbie messes up on her school project. Its first appearance was in Just Add Do-Overs.
It appears again in Just Add Tomorrow. This time, the girls use the spell to fix their day after Erin steals a pie tin from the Peizer exhibit. However, the spell repeated over twenty times before the girls are able to get out of the time loop.

Ingredients:

1. 3 tablespoons plain flour
2. Taurian Diablo Pepper
3. Dover Sole, scaled, cleaned, trimmed
4. Vegetable oil
5. Salt and freshly ground pepper

6. Sauce
7. 5 oz unsalted butter
8. 2 oz chopped fresh ginger root
9. About 3 limes worth lime juice
10. Chopped fresh cilantro

Directions

1. To prepare the fish, heat the oven to 400°F. Mix together the flour, chili powder and some salt & pepper, and dust the fish in it, then shake off any excess.

2. Add the oil and heat it until it hazes. Add sole and fry, without moving them, for 3-4 minutes until they form a golden crust. Turn over and transfer the frying pan to the top of hot oven and cook for a further 8-10 minutes until cooked through and the flesh is opaque.

3. Melt the butter in a frying pan and let bubble for 2-3 minutes. Reduce heat, add ginger, lime juice, and chopped cilantro and warm through.

4. Spoon over fish and serve.

Riddle:

Want to turn back time? You'll have to wait. This spell won't begin 'till you finish your plate.

Add 1 teaspoon of Taurian Diablo Pepper for every hour you want to repeat

Unscrambled Eggs

Unscrambled Eggs is a recipe in the Cookbook for cracking codes and solving for puzzles.

It's used by Kelly, Hannah, and Darbie in Just Add Codes in order to unlock the gate surrounding Chuck's secret cellar.

Ingredients:

1. 3 eggs or how much you want
2. 1/4 cup of milk
3. 1 pinch Galifrazian salt
4. 1 pinch Gründe pepper
5. 2 tsp butter

Directions

- Beat eggs, milk, Galifrazian salt and Gründe pepper in a medium bowl until blended.
- Heat butter in large nonstick skillet over medium heat until hot. Pour in egg mixture.
- As eggs begin to set, gently pull the eggs across the pan with a spatula forming large curds.
- Continue cooking - pulling, lifting and folding eggs - until thickened and no visible liquid egg remains.
- Stir constantly. Remove from heat. Serve immediately.

Riddle:

To crack a code, to find a link, change the way your brain can think. When all is solved, the spell is broken. 'Till then you'll think thoughts differently than spoken.

Walk through Wall-fles

Walk through Wall-fles was a spell mentioned and saw but was never used because the did not have any of the magic spices. It was seen in Just Add Barriers.

Ingredients:

- 2 cups Night Blooming flour
- 2 tablespoons sugar
- 1 tablespoon baking powder
- 1 teaspoon Galifrazian salt
- 1 3/4 cups milk
- 1/3 cup vegetable oil
- 1 egg

Directions

1. Combine the Night Blooming flour, sugar, baking powder, and Galifrazian salt in a mixing bowl.
2. Whisk the milk, vegetable oil, and egg together well in another bowl.
3. Gradually pour the milk mixture into dry mixture. Stir until it's almost blended. There will be a few lumps.
4. Pour the batter into your waffle maker (about 2/3 cup)and cook according to the instructions - approximately 4 - 6 minutes on medium high or until waffle maker stops steaming.

Riddle:

From one side of the wall to another, make sure what's on the other side is worth the bother.

Once you go into the desired room, you might not be able to leave soon.

Walk-In-My-Shoes Schnitzel

Walk-In-My-Shoes Schnitzel is a recipe cooked by Kelly to get out of the house while grounded to help Mama P and Jake cook Curse-Breaking Candied Stone Fruit for the Pluot Festival. Its first and only appearance was in Just Add Pluots.

Ingredients:

- Chicken Cutlets
- Eggs
- Flour
- Butter
- Bread Crumbs
- Elysian Salt
- Livonian Oil
- Parsley

Directions

1. Season chicken with salt and pepper.
2. Put flour on a plate. Beat eggs into shallow dish. Put bread crumbs in another shallow dish.
3. Take one piece of chicken and dredge in flour. Shake off the excess.
4. Drip egg yolk onto chicken
5. Carefully coat with bread crumbs and transfer to a baking sheet.
6. Heat oil and butter in a skillet.
7. When the oil is hot, put chicken in skillet and cook until golden brown.
8. Towel off excess oil and transfer chicken to plates.
9. Sprinkle with salt and pepper, and garnish with lemon and parsley.

Riddle:

When you need to have two faces, to be seen in two different places, have a friend pretend to be you.

Worst Party Ever Whipped Cream

Worst Party Ever Whipped Cream is a recipe cooked by Kelly in Just Add Surprise in order to spoil her party so that she could cook the Keep the Cookbook Casserole.

Ingredients:

- 1/2 teaspoon Merwaldian vanilla
- Strawberries (Qty of choice)
- 2 tablespoons Carnejian sugar
- 1 cup cold heavy whipping cream

Directions

Mix vanilla, whipping cream, and sugar until light, fluffy texture starts to take place. Place strawberries on top of whipped cream.

Riddle:

Make a party the worst you could wish, with all things fun erased. It will decline with just one dish, and end when all is embraced.

Copyright © 2024 by Barbara tom tom

All rights reserved. This book or any portion thereof may not be reproduced or used in any manner whatsoever without the express written permission of the publisher except for the use of brief quotations in a book review.

©Ursul tom Ursul

Manufactured by Amazon.ca
Acheson, AB